MW00678319

With Love
from
Eka & family
June 2, 1999

Everyday Prayer and Praise

CVP

Chariot Victor Publishing
A Division of Cook Communications

Chariot Victor Publishing,
a division of Cook Communications, Colorado Springs, CO 80918
Cook Communications, Paris, Ontario
Cook Communications, Eastbourne, England

EVERYDAY PRAYER AND PRAISE
© 1999 by David C. Cook Publishing Co.

Cover illustration by Debby Anderson
Cover design by Cheryl Ogletree

First printing, 1999
Printed in the United States of America
03 02 01 00 99   5 4 3 2 1

Table of Contents

Jesus said,
"Let the little children come to me,
and do not hinder them, for the king-
dom of God belongs to such as these.
I tell you the truth, anyone who will
not receive the kingdom of God like a
little child will never enter it."
Luke 18:16, 17 NIV

THANK YOU, JESUS

Dear Jesus,
Thank You for everything!

Thank You for
berries to pick.
Thank You for
fingers to lick.

Thank You for snow so cold.
Thank You for hands
to hold.

Thank You for the warm,
bright sun.
Thank You for room to run.

Thank You, Jesus,
for rocking chairs.
Thank You, Jesus,
for teddy bears.

Thank You for
a train to tug.
Thank You for
my grandpa's hug.

Thank You for
bunnies and puppies.
Thank You for
ducks and guppies.

Thank You for
a quiet night.
Thank You for
the moon so bright.

Thank You, Jesus,
for all I see.

Thank You for loving me.
In Jesus' name, Amen.

THREE CHEERS
FOR TODAY!

Good morning, Jesus!
It's a brand-new day.
I need to get up–
can't sleep it away!

Will it be sunny?
Will it be gray?
What will I do
with today?

Some days are for working;
I can help Mom or Dad.
Being a helper
will make me feel glad.

Some days are for playing,
for climbing a tree,

for splashing and dashing
and feeling free!

Some days are quiet, for
being still—

for thinking and praying
wherever I will.

Some days are happy,
some are sad,
but each is a special gift
from You, God.

So help me use it, not lose it.
It won't come by twice.

You made it, God, and it's
better than nice!
Thank You for today!
Amen.

This is the day the Lord has made;
let us rejoice and
be glad in it.
Psalm 118:24 NIV

A friend loves at all times.
Proverbs 17:17a NIV

FRIENDS

Thank You, Jesus,
for friends.

Friends trust me, even with their brand-new crayons.

Friends help me to try again.

Friends think
I am wonderful.

A friend is someone
I can pray for.

Jesus, You are my friend
forever and ever.

Friends love me anytime.

Friends forgive each other.

Friends take care
of each other.

Friends know
when I need a hug.

Thank You, Jesus,
for friends to love.
In Jesus' name, Amen.

TODAY IS
FOR TRUSTING

Dear Jesus,
It's good to know I can
always count on You.
You show me
which way to go.

One of your promises says,
"Trust in the Lord with all
your heart . . . and he will
show you the right way."
Proverbs 3:5, 6 TEV

Jesus, You help me
to be brave.

Your Word, the Bible, tells me, "I trust in God and am not afraid; I praise him for what he has promised."
Psalm 56:4 TEV

I know "You, Lord, give
perfect peace to those who
keep their purpose firm and
put their trust in you."
Isaiah 26:3 TEV

When I feel weak or tired, I remember the Bible verse that says, "Trust in the Lord God always, for in the Lord . . . is your everlasting strength." Isaiah 26:4 TLB

God, You make life
really special!
"Put [your] hope in God,
who richly provides us
with everything for
our enjoyment."
1 Timothy 6:17b NIV

I trust You, God, with
my whole heart . . .
because You love me and are
always watching out for me!

I trust in your unfailing
love; my heart rejoices
in your salvation.
Psalm 13:5 NIV
In Jesus Name, Amen.

Children are a gift from the Lord.
Babies are a reward.
Psalm 127:3 ICB

BABIES ARE FOR LOVING

Thank You, Jesus, for babies.
They are one of Your
best ideas!

Babies are quiet when
they're asleep.

Babies smile all over.

Babies like to
hold my hand.

Babies have a
lot to learn.

Babies smell so good—
when they are clean.

Babies are sometimes messy, soggy, and tired out.

Babies like to
do what I do.

Babies like to help
in the kitchen.

I'm glad You love
babies, Jesus.
In Jesus' name, Amen.

God, you have taught me
since I was young.
Psalm 71:17a ICB

HURRAY FOR
BIRTHDAYS!

Hurray, God!
It's my birthday!
I can't lose a birthday or
trade it; it's my very own.

It's free, but each year
I get only one.
Most people think it's
the best kind of fun.

It usually comes with good
things to eat . . .
sometimes with games and
candles and treats . . .

always with special family
and friends. . . .

I like it, God, when
my family sings to me!

I have just one birthday;
it shows up each year.

BIRTHDAY CERTIFICATE

_____

NAME

_____

BIRTH DATE

It's my day. I'm special
because You made me, God.
I'm one of a kind.
Before I was born,
You had me in mind.

*You saw me before I was born and
scheduled each day of my life before I
began to breathe. Every day was
recorded in your book!*
Psalm 139:16 TLB

You planned my birthday
before I was born,
so rat-a-tat, drum,
and tootle-toot, horn!

Hurray for birthdays!
In Jesus' name, Amen.

Teach us to number our days aright,
that we may gain a heart of wisdom.
Psalm 90:12 NIV

ALL YEAR LONG

Thank You for the seasons
of the year, Jesus.

Summer tastes like strawberries, cherry tomatoes, and ice cream.

You love me
in the summer, God.

Autumn is a good time
to lie in the leaves.

Autumn smells like
crayons, apples, and
new school shoes.

You love me in
the autumn, God.

Winter feels cold
on the outside and
warm on the inside.

Winter means making prints in fresh snow.

You love me in the winter, God.

Spring is a good time to
dance and play in
the warm grass.

Spring sounds like
quack-quack, cheep, baaa,
and happy giggles.

God, You love me in the
spring . . . and all year long.
In Jesus' name,
Amen.

Love is patient, love is kind. It does not envy, it does not boast, it is not proud.
It is not rude, it is not self-seeking, it is not easily angered, it keeps no record of wrongs. Love does not delight in evil but rejoices with the truth. It always protects, always trusts, always hopes, always perseveres. . . .
And now these three remain: faith, hope and love.
But the greatest of these is love.
I Corinthians 13:4-7, 13 NIV

LOVE IS KIND

If I don't have love, Jesus,
I am nothing.
Even if I were good and wise
and generous, it wouldn't
mean a thing without love.

Love is patient.
Love is kind.
Love isn't jealous.
Love doesn't brag.

Love isn't rude.
Love isn't selfish.
Love doesn't get mad easily.
Love doesn't keep
a list of wrongs.

Love is never happy about wrongdoing, but love is happy with truth.

Love always protects.
Love always trusts.

Love always hopes.
Love always keeps going.
Love never fails.

These three things
will last forever:
Faith,
Hope,
Love.
But the greatest
of these is love.

Help me to love others as
You have loved me, God.
In Jesus' name,
Amen.

Love the Lord your God with all your heart and with all your soul and with all your strength. These commandments that I give you today are to be upon your hearts. Impress them on your children. Talk about them when you sit at home and when you walk along the road, when you lie down and when you get up.
Deuteronomy 6:5-7 NIV

HOME IS BEST

Dear Jesus,
thank You for my home
and the lessons I learn there.

Home is where I learn
right from wrong.

Home is where there's room
to make mistakes.

Home is listening to music.
Thank You for music, Jesus.

Home is where
we listen to each other,
and share Your love, Jesus.

Home is the smell of buttered toast in the morning and clean sheets at night.

Home is the sound
of laughter and the taste of
popcorn. Thank You for fun
times with my family, Jesus.

Home is where
I am needed most.

Thank You, Jesus, that
home is where I belong.
In Jesus' name,
Amen.

Faith Parenting

Guide

Everyday Prayer and Praise

Age: 3-5

Life Issue: *My child doesn't know that prayer is simply talking to God.*
Spiritual Building Block: *Prayer*

Learning Styles

👁 *Visual Learning Style*

Spend time with your child looking for things to thank God for. Go to a park, take a walk, or simply lie in the grass and watch the clouds. See if your child can find scenes similar to those pictured in this book. Everywhere we look, we can find things for which to be thankful. Encourage your child to thank God for all things.

🔊 *Auditory Learning Style*

Read each prayer in this book to your child. Have him or her repeat the words back to you. Look for other prayers that you can read to your child, or even compose a prayer together that you can read and your child can repeat. Hearing you pray is the most effective way to teach your child to pray.

✋ *Tactile Learning Style*

Teach your child to pray by using a play telephone or a walkie-talkie. Talking to God is like talking to a friend on the phone. What things should we say to our Friend? Should we thank Him for the nice gifts He has given us? Should we ask for His help? Discuss these things. When your child feels more confident, try saying short prayers around the dinner table after a meal. Each person takes their turn creating something to tell God. This could include needs that the family or individuals have, praises for good things that have happened, or adoration to God for who He is.

Strengthen each day with prayer.

192